IN OTHER WORDS

by Matthew Seager

SAMUEL FRENCH

samuelfrench.co.uk

FOR PROFESSIONAL AND AMATEUR PRODUCTION ENQUIRIES

UNITED KINGDOM AND WORLD
EXCLUDING NORTH AMERICA
plays@samuelfrench.co.uk
020 7255 4302/01

UNITED STATES AND CANADA
info@samuelfrench.com
020 7255 4302/01

Each title is subject to availability from Samuel French, depending upon country of performance.

THINKING ABOUT PERFORMING A SHOW?

There are thousands of plays and musicals available to perform from Samuel French right now, and applying for a licence is easier and more affordable than you might think

---

From classic plays to brand new musicals, from monologues to epic dramas, there are shows for everyone.

Plays and musicals are protected by copyright law, so if you want to perform them, the first thing you'll need is a licence. This simple process helps support the playwright by ensuring they get paid for their work and means that you'll have the documents you need to stage the show in public.

Not all our shows are available to perform all the time, so it's important to check and apply for a licence before you start rehearsals or commit to doing the show.

LEARN MORE & FIND THOUSANDS OF SHOWS

Browse our full range of plays and musicals, and find out more about how to license a show

www.samuelfrench.co.uk/perform

Talk to the friendly experts in our Licensing team for advice on choosing a show and help with licensing

plays@samuelfrench.co.uk   020 7387 9373

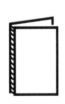
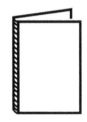

MUSIC USE NOTE

Licensees are solely responsible for obtaining formal written permission from copyright owners to use copyrighted music in the performance of this play and are strongly cautioned to do so. If no such permission is obtained by the licensee, then the licensee must use only original music that the licensee owns and controls. Licensees are solely responsible and liable for all music clearances and shall indemnify the copyright owners of the play(s) and their licensing agent, Samuel French, against any costs, expenses, losses and liabilities arising from the use of music by licensees. Please contact the appropriate music licensing authority in your territory for the rights to any incidental music.

USE OF COPYRIGHT MUSIC

A licence issued by Samuel French Ltd to perform this play does not include permission to use the incidental music specified in this copy.

Where the place of performance is already licensed by the PERFORMING RIGHT SOCIETY (PRS) a return of the music used must be made to them. If the place of performance is not so licensed then application should be made to the PRS, 2 Pancras Square, London, N1C 4AG.

A separate and additional licence from PHONOGRAPHIC PERFORMANCE LTD, 1 Upper James Street, London W1F 9DE (www.ppluk.com) is needed whenever commercial recordings are used.

IMPORTANT BILLING AND CREDIT REQUIREMENTS

If you have obtained performance rights to this title, please refer to your licensing agreement for important billing and credit requirements.

ABOUT THE AUTHOR

Matthew is a founding member and Artistic Director of Off the Middle theatre company. This is the first play he has written.

As an actor he has worked extensively in theatre across the UK and further afield. This includes multiple UK and international tours with Shakespeare company The HandleBards (*Hamlet; A Midsummer Night's Dream*) and with Blood of the Young (*Secret Show 1*; *Daphne Oram's Wonderful World of Sound*). He recently appeared as Marco Pantani in 2Magpies theatre company's production of *Ventoux*.

AUTHOR'S NOTE

As part of a module in my last year at the University of Leeds I was facilitating ten weeks of sensory stimulation workshops in a care home, Berkeley Court. We would work with residents suffering from dementia on different sensory exercises to see if any had a positive effect in terms of stimulating memories or general well-being. We decided to end each session by playing music. What we experienced was profoundly moving and, in many ways, life changing for me. Some residents who seemed completely cognitively unaware, distressed and unable to communicate coherently would stand and sing every word to a song they recognised from their childhood or young adult life. The resulting transformation in their mood or ability to remember and communicate was often astounding. It was equally both heartbreaking and beautiful, and resonated with me as a story that needed to be told. Our attempt is *In Other Words*.

There are many charities and organisations doing amazing work to raise awareness of Alzheimer's disease and other forms of dementia. Playlist for Life connect most closely with the topics explored in this play and we have been working with them since its first iteration. They use the music of a person's life to keep them connected to themselves and their loved ones throughout their dementia journey. The work they do is truly fantastic. Most recently they have collaborated with the BBC to launch the BBC Music Memories website.

Matthew Seager, January 2019

PRODUCTION NOTES

As stated by the Alzheimer's Association, it can be understood that there are seven stages of dementia, with the first being "no impairment" and the last "very severe decline". *In Other Words* loosely follows these criteria.

There are three "states" in this story to be aware of:

State 1: *Narrator state.* This is the world from which Arthur and Jane tell the story. They can jump into other states, but this is our base, the world they inhabit when addressing the audience. They are ageless, timeless versions of themselves. We are in their space. They are able to react to the flashbacks the audience have just seen, and can talk to them directly. We have previously called them "ghost characters" in rehearsal, which is by no means prescriptive but could be useful. Mostly they are relaxed, playful and totally connected when operating in this state.

State 2: *Flashback state.* We replay a scene from Arthur and Jane's life. They can snap back out into State 1 if they want to address the action or talk to the audience, but when in State 2 the fourth wall is up. Actors are expected to use their physicality, along with props, costume and other devices, to portray Arthur and Jane from the ages of around 30 to 80 years old.

State 3: *Dementia state.* These are unpleasant and increasingly disorientating moments in each stage/scene, designed to allow us to step inside Arthur's mind as his Alzheimer's worsens. We used sound and lighting to show Arthur's internal distress, confusion and distraction (including a Shotgun Condenser Microphone to distort the voice live). This increases in volume and abrasiveness as it appears during each scene, at particular moments when Arthur is seemingly becoming unreasonable or less responsive. This sound in each state would be based in the same "white noise" effect, but different, and a direct reaction to the environment Arthur is in at the time. For example, if he is in the street, the sound would be exaggerated with footsteps, the sound of cars, and voices. It is an attempt for us to experience what he is going through, and to allow us to make the connection between what is happening in reality, and how we are seeing him react.

IN OTHER WORDS

In Other Words was first presented at The Hope Theatre from 28 February to 18 March 2017 with the following cast and creatives:

ARTHUR – Matthew Seager
JANE – Celeste Dodwell

Producer – Matthew Seager/ Stephanie Withers/ Euan Tyre
for Off the Middle
Director – Paul Brotherston
Designer – Paul Brotherston
Assistant Director – Euan Tyre
Stage Manager – Stephanie Withers
Lighting Designer – William Alder
Sound Designer – Iida Aino
Dance Instructor – Romayne Etwaroo

The UK Tour of *In Other Words* ran from 7th February 2019 with the following cast and creatives:

ARTHUR – Matthew Seager
JANE – Angela Hardie

Producer – Tom Dixon for Off the Middle
Director – Paul Brotherston
Designer – Paul Brotherston
Technical Manager – Fergus Waldron
Lighting Designer – William Alder
Sound Designer – Iida Aino
Dance Instructor – Romayne Etwaroo

OFF THE MIDDLE

Matthew Seager – Artistic Director

Stephanie Withers – Executive Director

Euan Tyre – Development Director

Off the Middle was founded in 2016 by Matthew Seager, Stephanie Withers and Euan Tyre while they were studying at the University of Leeds. Here they discovered a shared passion for dynamic and innovative storytelling and have been making work together ever since.

They produce original new writing from members of the company and other emerging playwrights. Off the Middle's productions to date include:

In Other Words by Matthew Seager (The Hope Theatre/UK Tour)
Lead Suspect by Stephanie Withers (The King's Head Theatre)
Medicine by Meghan Tyler (The Hope Theatre)
Sam. The Good Person by Declan Perring (The Bunker Theatre)

www.offthemiddle.com / Twitter: @OTM_Theatre /
Facebook: /offthemiddle / Instagram: offthemiddle

CHARACTER LIST

ARTHUR
JANE

Any specific reference to nationality can be edited to fit the actor playing the role.

This script went to print during rehearsals, and may differ from the text in performance.

/ indicates interruption from the next character.
– indicates a self-interruption.
.... indicates hesitation or a trailing off of thought.

ACKNOWLEDGEMENTS

With thanks to Stephanie Withers, Euan Tyre, Arts Council England, Fiona Bell and the Bath and NE Somerset Dementia Action Alliance, Berkeley Court care home, University of Leeds, Royal Conservatoire of Scotland, The Arches, Andy Lowndes, Sarah Metcalfe and all at Playlist for Life, The Alzheimer's Society, The Lyric Hammersmith, The Hope Theatre, Geoffrey Owen, Christ Church & St Stephen Battersea, Eddy Hull, Clare Marcie, Samuel French Publishing and everyone else who has supported Off the Middle's productions.

For Mum, Dad, Lucy, Candy and Christa

As the audience enter, **ARTHUR** *and* **JANE** *are in the space.*
Casual and connected. **ARTHUR** *sits and* **JANE** *moves*
around. They untie **ARTHUR**'s *shoes and lay them by*
his chair. Eventually, **JANE** *places two wine glasses at*
upstage and downstage corners of the carpeted space.

On clearance, **ARTHUR** *tosses* **JANE** *her cardigan.*

"THAT'S LIFE" by Frank Sinatra* begins to play.

ARTHUR *and* **JANE** *age before our eyes. They become old.*
As **JANE** *turns to see* **ARTHUR**, *the music cuts out and*
is replaced by a ticking clock.

JANE *(as much to herself as to* **ARTHUR***)* Right. Shoes.

*(***JANE*** walks over to* **ARTHUR** *and begins to put his shoes*
on him.)

Come on, just let me... That's it... I just need to do this so
that we can get you ready to go out...

She struggles with this for a while. It's tough but familiar.
After some time **ARTHUR** *coughs and begins to strain*
and this evidently panics **JANE**.

It's ok – don't worry. We'll stop. Please don't... It's ok. Please.

JANE *lowers her head onto* **ARTHUR**'s *knee, exhausted.*
"SOMEWHERE BEYOND THE SEA" by Bobby Darin*
begins to play at the back of our hearing. **ARTHUR**
becomes young again and comforts **JANE**. *He invites*
her to dance. They stand. He takes her cardigan off and
they begin to dance together.

---

* For further information, please see Music Use Note on page v.

The dance ends with a dip/flourish, they spin off and pick up the glasses from the corner of the space. The music drifts into the background as if playing at a party. **ARTHUR** *and* **JANE** *bump into one another holding drinks.*

State 2:

ARTHUR Oh shit!

JANE Ah! ...Oh my God... *(wiping the drink off her)*

ARTHUR I am so, so sorry!

I can't believe it. I was just on my way to the bar to get a drink and...

Oh my God, you're covered.

JANE Yep.

ARTHUR What were you drinking?

JANE /Red

ARTHUR Oh God, that's going to stain, isn't it?

JANE Yes, I know.

ARTHUR I don't know what to say. I am so sorry, this was totally my fault/ I wasn't looking where I was going and—

JANE Well, obviously!

ARTHUR Sorry?

JANE Obviously it was your fault.

ARTHUR Oh of course, of course obviously, sorry.

I'm such an idiot!

Look, I'm really, really, really sorry.

A moment. We snap into State 1 – the music is gone, lighting changes. **ARTHUR** *is addressing the audience.*

So I know what you're thinking...that didn't start well.

JANE No, well you could say that.

ARTHUR And I can admit, you know, it certainly *looks* that way.

JANE *(exasperated)* Oh please, not this again.

ARTHUR But, no, I've said it before and I'll say it again. If I hadn't been so "clumsy", then you probably would have walked straight out that door, wouldn't you? So really it was a good thing, wasn't it? A perfectly calculated and masterfully executed romantic plan.

JANE Christ.

ARTHUR And that was it, you know. I knew. Straight away.

JANE Oh, shut up!

ARTHUR Hey, I did know! I mean, I don't know if you can *know*, you know...immediately, but now, looking back...

I knew.

JANE What *are* you talking about.

ARTHUR I mean that I...

Oh I don't know.

They snap immediately back into flashback, adopting the same pose as before.

State 2:

Let me get you a cloth, or a...a tissue or something?

JANE No, it's ok, I've got one, I think. *(pulls a tissue from her bra)*

ARTHUR Oh, ok.

Oh, but that's not enough tissue. I mean, for the amount of urmm...

I mean, you'll probably need some more tissue...

I'll just get you some more/ tissue

JANE Don't. It's fine.

ARTHUR Ok. Sorry, ok.

Another drink then? Please, at least let me buy you another drink?

JANE Honestly, it's fine. No need.

ARTHUR Please. Come on, it's the least I can do.

Pause.

JANE Ok then. Yes, fine.

ARTHUR Great, yes. Brilliant. What were you drinking?

JANE gestures to her top which, although it has nothing on it, to them is "obviously" covered in red wine.

Red wine! Red wine, of course. My fault. Red wine.

JANE You can stop saying it's your fault if you like.

ARTHUR Sorry, sorry. You're right.

JANE And sorry.

ARTHUR Right, yes of course. Sorr – I will.

JANE So English of you.

ARTHUR It is, isn't it? I hate that.

JANE Mmmmm.

ARTHUR Because you're obviously not from...urmm...

I mean, because you must be from...urmm...

JANE ...Scotland.

They snap out of flashback and address the audience.

ARTHUR And I remember thinking, right.

Scotland. Wow, that's... *(said seductively)* exotic.

JANE *(laughing)* Idiot.

They snap back into flashback.

ARTHUR Scotland. Wow, that's... *(said seductively)* exotic.

JANE Is it?

ARTHUR Yeah! Well, no. I mean, to me it is.

Because of...you know...the bagpipes and... haggis and stuff.

JANE ...Right.

And you are?

ARTHUR Yes of course. *(he holds out his hand)* Arthur.

JANE *(takes it)* Jane.

ARTHUR Hi.

JANE Hi.

Wine?

ARTHUR Mmm? Oh, wine, wine! Shit, sorry, sorry!

Well, no, I'm...I'm not sorry, because you told me to stop saying sorry. I mean, of course I am sorry, I'm just not saying it...apart now from I am.

Pause. **ARTHUR** *pulls his hand from hers.*

Sweaty hands...

Me, not you.

Snap out of flashback. State 1:

Jesus, was it really that bad? Can I just take this opportunity to say I do not remember it being that bad.

JANE Oh, but it really was.

ARTHUR It really was, wasn't it?

JANE I thought it was all part of the plan?

ARTHUR Well, yeah, of course it was. Maybe just with a little less, I don't know, verbal diarrhoea and sweating.

Still, it worked though, didn't it?

JANE I suppose it did, somehow.

ARTHUR You see Jane kissed me about two hours later.

JANE We kissed each other.

ARTHUR Yeah "ok", we kissed each other.

JANE We did!

ARTHUR Well, I mean, you went ninety, I went ten.

JANE God you're annoying.

> *They fall back into the chairs, snapping into flashback.*
> **JANE** *is wearing* **ARTHUR***'s jacket, which he gave her to cover up the wine stain. It is later in the same evening. They are getting on.* **ARTHUR** *has seemingly recovered from his previous awkwardness and is more confident.*

> **JANE** *is laughing. State 2:*

ARTHUR Ah, so that's it, is it.

JANE That's what?

ARTHUR I've done it!

JANE Done what?

ARTHUR I've figured it out.

JANE You've lost me.

ARTHUR The number of drinks I needed to buy for you to forgive me and forget about the... *(he gestures to her top)* incident.

JANE The incident... I like it.

ARTHUR Thanks.

JANE Mysterious.

ARTHUR Yes, well, that's me.

JANE Oh, is it really?

ARTHUR Yeah. Can't you tell?

JANE No comment. And I hadn't forgotten.

ARTHUR Yes you had.

JANE No I hadn't. I was...temporarily distracted.

ARTHUR I'll take it.

JANE And it's only because you said the jacket covers it.

ARTHUR I said it looks like part of the top. It's...stylish, you know. I know about these things.

JANE Stylish *and* mysterious.

They laugh.

Well, you're wrong then. About the number of drinks.

ARTHUR Am I?

JANE Yes. It's one more.

ARTHUR Then I'm forgiven?

JANE Then you're forgiven.

ARTHUR Deal.

JANE Make it something exotic. You know...like me.

ARTHUR *(embarrassed)* Very funny.

He laughs. She laughs.

Definitely a moment.

"FLY ME TO THE MOON"* has come on in the background. They finish laughing and share a moment in silence, enough for us to hear the song and enjoy it.

First will...you, I mean, do you want to...urmm...

It's just...I love this song, you know, and it feels a lot like I want to ask/ so I was just—

JANE Ah God, me too!

---

* For further information, please see Music Use Note on page v.

ARTHUR What?

JANE Love this song.

ARTHUR Oh, great! Yeah it's...it's great, isn't it?

Do you want to dance with me?

JANE ...Absolutely

ARTHUR Oh...right...good...

They dance – they enjoy the song. **ARTHUR** *spins her as a bit of a joke. When they re-embrace they are closer. The music begins to get louder as* **JANE** *moves closer to kiss* **ARTHUR**. *Just as they are about to kiss they snap out of flashback.*

State 1:

I told you! I told you. You went nintey, and I went ten!

JANE Oh my – you are unbelievable.

ARTHUR And actually, it was then. That's when I knew. Not earlier, not when I said it earlier. It was then...that moment.

JANE Yeah ok. Me too.

They kiss.

ARTHUR You see, I'd always fancied myself as a bit of a Sinatra – and that song, at a moment like that.

(to audience) Well, it just doesn't get much more perfect, does it?

(to her) We didn't stand a chance.

They embrace and spin out in a dance move with extension. Background music snaps in. **JANE** *is putting on earrings,* **ARTHUR** *is reading the paper.*

Stage 1: No Impairment

Flashback – Apartment. State 2:

JANE We should go.

ARTHUR Mmmm.

JANE Like...now.

ARTHUR ...I agree.

JANE You're not moving.

ARTHUR Neither are you.

JANE Do you even know what time it is?

ARTHUR Yes.

JANE Are you sure?

ARTHUR Of course.

JANE Well then?

ARTHUR It's urm...

> ARTHUR *tries to subtly look at his watch.*

JANE Shut up. The reservation's in twenty minutes, we're going to be late.

ARTHUR Well, I guess we'll just be late then

> *He gets up and pulls her into a dance.*

JANE But we agreed we'd get there for nine. That's late enough as it is, if you didn't want to go that's fine, it's not like I mind, we should have just not booked it in the first place, I—

ARTHUR *(laughing)* Will you shut up.

JANE It's not funny, we're going to be late.

ARTHUR Well, stop dancing then.

> *Pause.*

JANE I don't want to.

ARTHUR We could go out and waste money on overpriced food any day we wanted. Why ruin tonight by doing it?

JANE *(smiling)* Because I'm hungry.

ARTHUR Yeah me too.

Pause.

Maybe we should go out for dinner?

JANE *hits him playfully.*

Hey!

JANE Well, I'm going. It's your choice whether you come with me or not.

ARTHUR I have a choice? You should have told me that before. In that case, I'll put my feet up.

JANE *(joking)* I'm so glad I married you.

ARTHUR *(sincerely)* Me too.

We let this moment sit. "FLY ME TO THE MOON"* comes on the radio/playlist. They hear it.

First, would you urmm... I mean, do you want to.

JANE *recognises the game.*

It's just...I love this song, you know, and it feels a lot like I want to/ ask.

JANE Stop it...

ARTHUR Do you want to dance with me?

JANE Absolutely...not.

They get up and dance.

ARTHUR *begins to sing along to the music.**

---

* For further information, please see Music Use Note on page v.

Don't ruin it.

ARTHUR Right.

They hold the dance and the music may swell before we snap out of flashback. They break the embrace in State 1. ARTHUR *begins to move the chairs and arrange cushions.*

JANE *(to audience)* It makes me smile whenever I think about it. Cheers me up. Always will, I think.

He'd play that song whenever he did something wrong. Knows I can't stay angry. I can't, honestly. And he always had such an...awful voice.

ARTHUR Bit harsh.

JANE It just seemed strange, I suppose.

Both his parents were such good singers. So beautiful – his whole family really. And he should have been as well, but...

Scientists have done these tests, you see, and this is real scientific published research.

And it says that the second we're born our cries mimic the tone and rhythm, even the accent actually, of our mother.

So in my head, I mean, before we're even born, effectively, we're learning to sing with another person, aren't we?

Isn't that amazing.

And he still sounded that bad.

I think, oddly, that was happiest I've ever been, in a way. That evening.

ARTHUR Me too. We never did make it out for dinner...if you know what I mean.

JANE I think they all know what you mean, Arthur.

ARTHUR *has finished placing cushions on the chairs and moving them slightly.*

It looked like that, didn't it, for years?

ARTHUR *(mischievously)* Mmmm... Are you sure this wasn't... there? And are you sure this wasn't there? *(putting it back)*

JANE Stop it! It's not much...

> **ARTHUR** *spins* **JANE** *to sitting and sits down himself, opening a newspaper.*

ARTHUR You can say that again.

JANE But it was ours.

> *They have aged a little. Snap into flashback.*

Stage 2: Very Mild Decline

State 2:

JANE *writes Christmas cards and* **ARTHUR** *reads the paper – Christmas as usual.*

JANE What was that?

ARTHUR I didn't say anything.

JANE Oh...oh sorry.

I just thought I heard you say you were going to make a cup of tea, that's all...strange.

ARTHUR *looks up from his paper, and around their kitchen.*

ARTHUR Fine.

JANE What?

ARTHUR Would you like a cup of tea, Jane?

JANE Oh really? Yeah! That'd be great, thanks.

ARTHUR *gets up.*

You'll need to go to the shops and buy some milk though, we've run out.

ARTHUR Oh. I see.

ARTHUR *puts on a scarf and turns to leave.*

JANE Oh and whilst you're at it, we need some stamps. Got to get these sent.

ARTHUR Anything else, your highness?

JANE No, that'll be all... You're dismissed.

ARTHUR *turns to face the front – as he does so the Christmas music cuts out, he is addressing the audience. State 1:*

ARTHUR I suppose in hindsight I think this was probably the start. Not because of what happened, but because of what kept happening after this happened, you know?

I mean, milk and stamps – MILK AND FUCKING STAMPS – doesn't get much easier than that, right?

It's less than a five-minute walk to the shops from our front door. I've timed it.

Three minutes in there, if there's no queue. Which, I remember, there wasn't... Ironic, I suppose...

Anyway, three minutes in there, then five minutes home.

That's less than a fifteen-minute round trip. Easy.

So I got to the shops...

We faintly hear and see our first State 3 – ARTHUR *reacts to it, apparently losing his train of thought.*

To buy... The...urr...urmm items...

...

And just stood there.

Snap out of State 3. State 1:

JANE There was no way that it took him half an hour to get milk and stamps from the shops. It's less than five minutes away. *(sighs)* He's timed it.

I'm not sure, but I think I thought he was trying to get out of writing the Christmas cards. Every year. As if I'd have let him write them anyway.

Once you're an "expert". Once you've been through it, you kick yourself for not noticing the seemingly endless list of "obvious" things. Staring you right in the face. I know I did.

But they're not, of course they're not. It's the last thing you think about. Why should you? It would have been impossible to connect this with...everything...impossible... I know that.

But then again, I think it's equally impossible to not blame yourself for missing it. If that makes sense?

But we'll get to that later... Half an hour.

ARTHUR Half an hour it took me, round trip. Five fucking minutes I stood there without a clue. Blank. Couldn't have picked milk and stamps out of a line up.

I sort of floated back home. I was so...detached. Like I was watching myself.

As I got back to our front door, I mean right to the front door, the lights just went back on. *(clicks his fingers)* All came back to me.

And so I marched back to the shops, grabbed my milk and stamps, victorious. It'd been a long day. I'm a forgetful person. Right? This was just a sign of getting a little older and a little tired-er.

Look – I'm sure it happens to all of you occasionally. So trivial, isn't it? A middle-aged man forgetting what to buy from the shops?

But that's just it. If it had only been occasionally, I probably wouldn't even have remembered that "this" happened. But After "this", it started to not only be "occasionally" – anymore.

No one else noticed at first, of course. Why should they? Like I said, "trivial".

ARTHUR *snaps back to face* JANE *and the Christmas music comes on – State 2:*

JANE *(without even looking up from her task)* Took your time, didn't you...?

ARTHUR Oh really, urrrrm yeah *(trying to cover up)*. Yeah, sorry about that. I, urmm/ I—

JANE *(laughing)* Well, you know how to make it up to me, don't you.

ARTHUR *(smiling)* I'll put the kettle on.

ARTHUR *looks to the audience. Music cuts out.* JANE *looks at him with a pained expression. State 1:*

I know Jane thinks she should have picked up on it. Thinks it could have made some kind of difference. Which is ridiculous. How were you meant to know if I didn't even have a clue?

I don't know –

It went on like that for ages. Years actually. An unexplained fall. Cuts and bruises. The fog slowly beginning to descend. I kept trying to cover it up and life just kept happening, you know.

ARTHUR *spins* JANE *up from the chair, facing her.*

I'm sorry.

Anyway, like I said – I think that was the beginning.

Slight moment of dance move with extension and snap into flashback.

They have aged again.

We have evidently joined the flashback in the middle of an argument. ARTHUR *has lost the keys.*

Stage 3: Mild Decline

State 2:

JANE Have you checked the pot by the front door?

ARTHUR Of course I have!

JANE How about the drawer in your bedside table?

ARTHUR They are *not* there!

JANE Look, Arthur! You had them last, I know you did!

ARTHUR I can't have. You can't be sure. Let's just think, shall we?

JANE I am sure! Can you just think? You went to the shops, you had lost them, again, so I lent you mine *(looks at her watch)*, and now we're late, and it's important—

ARTHUR Again? What do you mean again? How is that helping? That's not going to help, is it?

JANE Alright ok. Ok ok. Will you just try to relax and think?

ARTHUR Oh, try and think. Oh, see, I wasn't thinking, and now you've told me to think, we'll be able to find them much more easily.

JANE Fantastic! Brilliant, great work, Arthur.

ARTHUR Well, thank you very much, Jane, because everything else is my fucking fault.

JANE What do you mean, everything else! I'm not talking about *anything* else – I'm talking about this—

ARTHUR *(frustrated with himself)* You're not even going to entertain the possibility, for a second, that you could have lost the keys?

JANE NO! I'm not, Arthur. You know it was you and you know that I am not being unreasonable!

We begin to enter State 3 for the second time, slightly louder and for slightly longer this time, making **ARTHUR** *distracted and struggling to find his words.*

When did you have them last?

ARTHUR What...?

Have what?

JANE What do you mean what? Are you joking?

...THE KEYS

ARTHUR ...Yes...yes, I know that. Last time I had them I... Well, I got home and...they were...urmm...they were...

JANE Where?

ARTHUR On the...they were on the...

JANE What?

Snap back into State 2, and **ARTHUR** *finds the word immediately and over forcefully.*

ARTHUR Table! They were on the kitchen table!

JANE *(looking at table)* Lovely! Well they're not there now are/ they...

ARTHUR I'm just saying that they *were* on the/ table.

JANE And now we've missed it.

ARTHUR GOOD! I DIDN'T WANT TO FUCKING GO ANYWAY!

Long silence, **ARTHUR** *is furious. We slowly see this drain away, replaced by guilt.*

I'm sorry.

JANE *shakes her head.*

Hey. Hey, I'm sorry, ok.

JANE *ignores* ARTHUR *and he walks over to the radio/ CD player. Presses play.* **"FLY ME TO THE MOON"** *comes on. He dances over to her in a silly way. She can't help but give in and laughs. This is their song.*

They are now dancing together.

ARTHUR *begins to sing.*

JANE Don't ruin it.

ARTHUR Right.

They dance with each other.

I am sorry, you know.

JANE I know.

Are you ok?

ARTHUR I'm fine. I'm just...tired, stressed.

Feeling a bit run down. That's all.

JANE Still?

ARTHUR Yes, I know.

I know.

JANE Will you please go to the doctor?

ARTHUR I just need a bit of TLC, that's all.

JANE Just fucking go to the doctor, Arthur!

ARTHUR Ok.

JANE Thank you.

ARTHUR I'm fine, but ok.

Snap to State 1.

---

* For further information, please see Music Use Note on page v.

JANE Turns out he had forgotten that he'd driven into town that morning, locked the car and walked home. I found his keys in the fridge an hour later.

I was getting some milk to make a cup of tea.

ARTHUR Well, it does sound bad when you put it like that.

JANE He didn't complain about being tired much. Or stressed. He never really complained at all.

It was one of the things that amazed me about you. But now, well...

I thought he was getting the flu.

ARTHUR I thought I was getting the flu. Or something. For a bit. So did the doctor actually, at first. Then it was, "Perhaps you're just slowing down slightly, Arthur. As we all do."

But it wasn't their fault. Or maybe it was. I don't know.

They asked me to bring Jane with when they did tests, so they could ask her questions, I suppose.

But she didn't know. I didn't tell her.

Told myself there was no point in worrying her unless there was definitely something to worry about, you know.

JANE So stupid/.

ARTHUR Yes, anyway. Eventually the doctor. Well...

JANE *slowly moves the chair forward, and* ARTHUR *sits down, snapping into a doctor's appointment.* JANE *is at the other chair reading from a doctor's letter. The two scenes sync up.* JANE*'s reading of the doctor's letter becomes* ARTHUR *receiving the news.*

What's the damage then, doctor?

JANE Your results indicate that you are showing signs of Mild Cognitive Impairment – or MCI. Now, there are different types of MCI, the most common being Amnestic, in which the patient, such as yourself, shows abnormal signs of memory loss in relation to age, but other cognitive functioning is occurring at a normal rate. On average, twenty per cent of those with MCI will go on to develop a form of dementia. With Amnestic Mild Cognitive Impairment, this would most likely be Alzheimer's disease. Our next step is to refer you to a specialist, so you can have an MRI scan, which will decipher the possible levels of amyloid protein that have built up on the outside of the nerve cells in your brain, causing toxic plaques...

During the above, after the word "Alzheimer's", ARTHUR stands and pushes the chair back into the home positions. He has returned from the appointment. When he sits we snap into State 2. It is later the same day.

Stage 4: Moderate Decline

State 2 flashback:

JANE *is standing reading from a booklet of papers.*
ARTHUR *is sitting.*

JANE Why didn't you tell me sooner?

Arthur!

ARTHUR There was nothing to tell.

JANE Of course there is.

ARTHUR Yes, I know there is now.

I'm saying there wasn't before. Not really.

JANE That's just not true, Arthur. Is it?

JANE *is looking through the papers.*

ARTHUR /Ok.

JANE All of this. It all emphasises the importance of making
changes as early as possible./ That's the only way—

ARTHUR Ok, I said ok! Jesus, what do you want me to say? I'm
just trying process it all.

JANE Arthur, twenty per cent of people really isn't that much,
and it says it here that there's a good chance that all this
is being caused by something completely different. Look:

She reads from the paper.

"In approximately twenty per cent of cases, Mild Cognitive
Impairment will lead to a form of..." – well. Yes... "but in
the remainder of cases, it can be caused by any number
of internal or external factors. These can include, anxiety,
stress—"

Well, that sounds familiar, doesn't it?

Look. What I'm trying to say is if we just focus on what we can be doing to help, because, I mean, we can only control what we can control, you know?

Pause.

...And then it probably won't even get to/ that

ARTHUR It might.

JANE I'm trying to be/ positive.

ARTHUR I know. I know. I'm sorry.

JANE Don't be. Really.

ARTHUR I know. But I am. About it all.

This could be...

JANE Don't.

ARTHUR I mean, you didn't sign up for this./ This isn't fair.

JANE Shut/ up.

ARTHUR This isn't fair on us.

JANE It's not. So what?

ARTHUR You're right. You're right, as always. Dangerous to think like that. I know.

I can get through it. I know I can/ it's just...

JANE We can get through it.

Have you read these?

ARTHUR *(smiles)* Have you?

JANE Yes, I have. With Mild Cognitive Impairment, your "condition" is more likely to worsen if you live by yourself, see *(gestures to one of the pieces of paper)* because then you don't have "sufficient stimulation in your home environment".

ARTHUR *(laughing at the sexual nature of the reference)* Well, I have to say at first I was sceptical, but that's definitely something I'm open to.

JANE Very funny, concentrate. This is important. I mean people to talk to, you know. Social events.

So, I was thinking, I mean, we'll see how you are at the time, but let's have a big group over for your birthday, a proper dinner, what do you think?

ARTHUR I've just had my birthday, I don't need to start planning –

Right. Ok. Sounds good.

JANE Good.

ARTHUR Great.

JANE *(looking at the papers)* And it says having "substantial and topical conversations are important factors in keeping your brain fit and healthy".

ARTHUR *looks confused.*

ARTHUR "Substantial and topical"?

JANE Oh I don't know, discussions – current affairs and things.

ARTHUR Oh, yeah, well, it's a good thing we have so many of those then...

JANE Well, we're going to start now, aren't we!

ARTHUR *(laughing)* Are we?

Sorry, you're right, you're right. Maybe we should just skip straight to "stimulating my home environment"?

JANE *(annoyed)* Hilarious.

ARTHUR *(sincere)* Thank you.

JANE It's not a compliment. You need to take this seriously/ you know, for God's sake.

ARTHUR No, I mean/ thank you for ev—

JANE Your way of dealing with this might be to tell jokes but it's not mine, and I'm sorry for sounding selfish, but this is about me as well, ok. And I think it's going to be really, really fucking difficult/ and I'm not sure we quite realise how hard, but—

ARTHUR Hey, I was being serious. I meant it, ok...I meant it. Thank you.

You think I'm not scared? Do you think this fucking huge giant possibility doesn't terrify me?

Of course it does. Can you imagine what I'd be like without you here?

I'm not sure I'd cope.

JANE *(smiling)* You wouldn't.

Snap out of State 2 and into State 1.

Doesn't seem fair, does it? The hardest and most important thing to do is admit that there may be a problem, and then the second you do, that's the exact moment that it starts to escalate. Maybe accepting the problem is a form of admitting defeat.

Snap into State 2. We are still in Stage 4 of the disease.

JANE *is standing and* ARTHUR *is sitting:*

I think we should put Sue next to Graham, they've always got on, don't you think?

ARTHUR Yes, yes of course, why not. *(writes on the paper)*

JANE Or maybe not because Angela never liked them being too close, she's a bit funny about that?

ARTHUR Is she?

JANE Sue can be a bit...

ARTHUR Well, ok. *(scribbles out on the paper)*

JANE But I suppose Angela's insecurities shouldn't dictate where we put Graham, should they.

ARTHUR *(slightly exasperated)* no, no I suppose not.

State 3 again, distracting and confusing **ARTHUR**. *Starting quietly but slowly getting louder and louder as* **JANE** *becomes more frantic and eventually angry. We are inside* **ARTHUR**'s *head.*

JANE Who do you think Angela should go next to?

Silence – **ARTHUR** *is confused.*

Arthur?

ARTHUR Oh. Right, yes, yes I'll put that down now.

JANE Put what down, I asked you who you thought Angela should go next to?

ARTHUR I thought we'd agreed, didn't we? Angela's/ going—

JANE Oh, before I forget, did you reply to that letter from the bank by the way?

ARTHUR What?

JANE It's not a problem if you haven't. It's just that I was going to do it and you said that you were just about to do it, so?

ARTHUR Urrm yes, yes/ I remember.

JANE So you have done it or you are going to do it?

ARTHUR What, no, I said I've done it/ I think.

JANE But we can't put Angela next to him.

ARTHUR Sorry, next/ to who?

JANE Oh great, you did pay/ it then?

ARTHUR Sorry, are we talking about Angela or not, because I really couldn't care less who she/ sits next to?

JANE You didn't pay/ it, why?

ARTHUR I said I did, I think/ I did.

JANE You want to put Angela next to David?/ Are you joking, Arthur?

ARTHUR David, who is David?/ Jane, please slow down.

JANE Who is Angela? What do you mean who is Angela/, my sister Angela?

ARTHUR Yes of course I know that/ I was talking about the bills, about the bank!

JANE You didn't pay Angela?/ you said you did!

ARTHUR I was meant to pay Angela? What do you mean? You never asked me to.

JANE What have you done?/ This is serious Arthur!

ARTHUR What do you mean, what have I done?/ I don't understand, what are we talking about.

JANE WHAT THE HELL HAVE YOU DONE?/ I can't believe you, Arthur!

ARTHUR Look, can we just/ take a break, please, Jane?

JANE (aggressively) I can't believe you, Arthur?!

ARTHUR Can you just stop.

JANE (aggressively) Arthur?!

ARTHUR Can you just calm down? STOP FOR ONE FUCKING MOMENT!

JANE (repeats angrily) ARTHUR!

State 3 reaches a loud crescendo and cuts out suddenly. **JANE** *is still repeating "Arthur", but now in a concerned fashion. It is apparent to the audience that we have just gained an insight into* **ARTHUR***'s mind. Her anger and aggression is delusion manifested by* **ARTHUR***'s brain.*

She is concerned but he continues, angry and upset. State 2.

(repeats with concern) Arthur.

ARTHUR Why won't you listen to me? Just stop!!

JANE Stop what?

ARTHUR Calm down!!

JANE I'm completely calm. I just want to try and help/ you understand.

ARTHUR WILL YOU JUST STOP FUCKING HASSLING ME FOR ONE SECOND!

JANE I haven't been hassling/ you.

ARTHUR Of course you are! How can you look me in the eye and say that? Leave me alone. Please.

JANE I've done nothing...

ARTHUR I SAID LEAVE ME ALONE!

Long silence. It is apparent that this is the worst episode they've had.

*Eventually he goes over to the CD player and puts on **"FLY ME TO THE MOON"***. **JANE** walks towards him and he is hopeful, but this time she turns it off immediately. It's gone too far this time.*

JANE I'm not angry. Not at you.

We just need more help.

ARTHUR It feels like I am breaking.

JANE I know. I understand, ok. Well, I don't – but I want to.

*Snap into State 1. During the following, **JANE** moves the chairs so that they are side by side, facing front.*

ARTHUR I didn't understand either. No one did actually. It was two scans and three appointments before we were finally

---

* For further information, please see Music Use Note on page v.

referred to a specialist. It's ironic in a way. Doctors spend so much time asking you to put these thoughts into words, when what it is doing is taking away your ability to think, you know. And all the time you're just living with it. You wake up each morning not sure which version of yourself you're going to be, or if another part of you might have fallen away.

ARTHUR *sits and we snap into State 2. An appointment with the specialist. They have aged.*

Stage 5: Moderately Severe Decline

The doctor is a fixed point ahead. During this stage an "..." at the beginning of the line indicates the doctor is speaking.

ARTHUR Hi there, doc. How are you?

...Oh good good.

...How do *I* think I'm doing? Well. I'm not sure. Not great obviously. That's the thing, you see, I'm not sure.

I like to think of it as if some days the sun shines and some days it rains, you know.

Yeah, and on a sunny day it's like... I can see for miles. Everything is clear. It makes sense. Definitely seems to be winter, at the moment.

There are things that I know, and there are things that I know that I know, but often, when it really gets down to it, you know, I can't quite get them. Tip of the tongue.

JANE Yes, I think that's fair.

ARTHUR ...Right, ok.

..."Apple. Labrador. Grass, apple, Labrador, grass." *(laughing)* It's like the bloody generation game, this. Urm. Yes, ok, I'll try.

...You mean, now, right here.

Well. We are in a hospital.

...And urmmm – it is a Tuesday.

... *(looks confused)* Words? Words? Oh yes! The words I do, yes I do remember. Of course, apple...Labrador (ARTHUR *struggles with this last one but finds it eventually.)*, grass.

...Ok. Thanks.

JANE Thanks Doctor.

ARTHUR See you next time.

We snap into State 3, showing the passing of time and ARTHUR's *continued decline. We hear sounds of the hospital.* JANE *puts a scarf onto* ARTHUR *and they sit down. We snap into State 2.*

JANE Hi, doctor, how are you?

...Good good, I'm fine thanks.

ARTHUR Hi there.

...Please, fire away!

...Well. I don't think so, no.

(frustrated) I'm sorry. I know I have seen you before because Jane told me. And the name, Jameson, yes of course, the name. But not the face. Not at all...

How is that possible... Sorry.

JANE Hey, that's ok. There's nothing to be sorry about.

ARTHUR ... "Apple. Labrador. Grass." – ok, yes, I'll do my best.

...Recently? Well, feel like I might get lost on the way to the bathroom, some days.

And I have done *(chuckles)*.

I tell you what. I don't know how people do this on their own *(holds* JANE's *hand and doesn't let go)*. She keeps me going. I'm sure about that.

...Ok, yes. We are in a...urmm. We are. Well. We are in the urmm.

In the building that we...come to see you in, doctor. *(trying to make a joke of it)* Sorry.

...Day of the week? Oh, well, I'm afraid that might be pushing it.

(working it out in his head) No wait, I know – it's a Wednesday, isn't it? *(evidently a guess)*

(covering) Oh yes! Of course, of course it's Monday.

(blank look and long pause) Oh yes. Yes, yes I do remember.

Apple...urrm uhh... La...brador... *(can't get the last one, gets very frustrated)* Sorry.

JANE It's ok, it's fine, you did your best.

ARTHUR ...Yes that's fine, I'll just wait here.

__JANE__ stands and is talking to the doctor alone outside. __ARTHUR__ relaxes into State 1.

JANE ...Me? *(not expecting this question)* Yes I'm fine, I suppose.

It's day-to-day things now, you see. I have to pick his clothes out for him some days. He can't really...get the right order.

The other day, in the morning after his alarm went off – he's worst in the mornings, you see, before he's properly woken up. Anyway, his alarm went off, and I had to remind him what to do next. I mean the next action.

To sit up and get out of bed.

...Yes, it's hard work.

My husband is becoming more like a child and less like my husband every day.

I get so...angry. So frustrated. And then I get angry at myself for being angry, which means I can't do my job properly – *(laughs)* and that's what it's starting to become now. It's my job...

It feels... it feels like he's leaving me, you know.

...Yes, yes. I'll be fine. Let's go back in.

__ARTHUR__ moves back into State 2 as __JANE__ turns round.

ARTHUR ...Oh ok, thank you. See you then.

JANE Bye, doctor.

We snap into State 3 again, showing __ARTHUR__'s decline. __JANE__ takes a cushion from one chair and helps __ARTHUR__ to sit. As she does so we snap into State 2, only this time the lights change but the sound remains distorted. Lines are becoming blurred.

Hi, doctor.

...I'm good thanks, and you?

...Good, good.

State 3 again, loudly – we are inside his head.

ARTHUR *(distressed)* I don't need you to come with me, you know. I can do it on my own. I don't want to be here. I don't want her here!

JANE Well, that's not very nice, is it, Arthur. I'm only here to help. As you can see, he's being quite difficult today, doctor?

ARTHUR You know she won't let me leave the house. Keeping me prisoner in my own fucking home.

...Questions?!

Becomes suspicious...

...Why?

...WHY?! Why should I wait here, what do you need to talk about? *(accusing the doctor)* You're part of this, aren't you?!

JANE *(menacing)* Come on now Arthur, why don't you...just...

Snap out of State 3. State 2. JANE *is concerned.*

...Just calm down, Arthur. Please, it's ok. The doctor just wants to ask me a few questions.

ARTHUR You're such a...pest, you know. A horrible woman... nasty...bitch...that's what you are – a fucking horrible bitch.

JANE ...I'll be right back.

ARTHUR *(muttering to himself)*...Prisoner in my own fucking home.

JANE *steps outside,* ARTHUR *relaxes into State 1 again.*

JANE ...Much worse. Almost by the day now, or that's what it feels like.

He's furious because I wouldn't let him drive here. Surely he knows that he can't get here by himself.

...No. No you're right...of course not.

He can be so unkind.

...No, God no, never physically. And I know it's not him when he's like that, but it's...

Can I tell you something... I mean, I feel like I need to tell someone, so I'd really like to tell you, I think.

He likes baths, you see, feels nice, I think, the water. It's quiet for him. Sometimes I need to help him wash, or to remind him to get out when he's finished...

It was urmm last Tuesday, or...or Monday maybe, it doesn't matter. He was in the bath, I was sitting on the edge, singing to him...well, humming, singing, whistling, kind of an awful mixture of the three. It was our song though, God he loves that, it's one of the only things that reminds me it's him sometimes.

He was lying back with his eyes closed, and you might think he was asleep but there was this faint twitch on the corners of his lips. The beginnings of a smile, I think, I don't know, and if you really listened quietly, it was like he was humming, humming but without sound, if that makes sense? Anyway – he was content, you know, or as content as you can be.

I thought to myself, right there, very seriously...push him under...fucking push him under and...and I imagined doing it... I felt the struggle... I saw the last bubble wriggling out of his mouth, vanishing on the surface...then stillness...and I smiled.

I closed my eyes and thought...let him die, now, listening to me sing our song, with his eyes closed, and the beginnings of a smile on his face, and let me be the one to do it.

...No, today's not a good day. Today is not a good day.

JANE *turns to go back in but is so distressed that we snap into State 1.*

Arthur, sorry.

Oh – it was so hard.

It was so hard.

Sorry.

ARTHUR Ok. It's ok.

They share a moment.

JANE Alright.

ARTHUR You sure?

JANE *nods.*

JANE Yeah.

ARTHUR Ok then.

Snap to State 2. Final doctor's appointment. ARTHUR *looks happy – almost childlike.*

JANE Hi, doctor.

...Yes, fine thanks.

ARTHUR ...Yes please, fire away, doctor.

...Oh yes well. I think things are going pretty well, thanks. It feels, you know, not bad. Yes, it feels not bad, I'd say, just the same, you know.

He genuinely thinks this.

JANE Well, I'm not sure about that, Arthur.

ARTHUR *chuckles vacantly and openly.*

ARTHUR ...Sorry? Oh...what was that? "Apple, Labrador, grass"?

Apple...Labrador...grass...

Apple... M m m.aplole

l.l.label Ga.uh.gr...gra

ARTHUR *forgets them as he is saying them.*

Oh. Oh. Forgotten them already. *(confused)*

JANE ...You got lost in our back garden yesterday, didn't you, Arthur? Always looking for some woman. He says, "looks upset", talks to her sometimes.

Laughing.

Oh, no I know. I shouldn't be.

But if I don't laugh about it, I'm not sure what I'll do.

...Oh wow. Right, *(trying to be strong)* ok, well, I really wasn't expecting that, you know. I mean, really that feels quite soon.

You're saying not at all?

...Oh ok. I understand

Thanks, doctor. Thank you. Come on, Arthur, time to go.

ARTHUR Time to go!

JANE We'll see you next time.

We snap into State 3, again showing ARTHUR's *ageing and decline.* JANE *rearranges the chairs. Canned laughter seeps into the State 3 soundscape.* ARTHUR *sits and* JANE *produces a tea cup from the chair.*

We snap into State 2. Canned laughter is heard straight away from the TV.

ARTHUR *watches the television. He laughs.*

ARTHUR This is funny. I do like this one. Have you seen it?

JANE Yes. Yes, Arthur, I like watching this one with you.

He laughs again.

What vegetables would you like with your chicken, Arthur? I was thinking I'd do pea's.

He looks at her.

ARTHUR (*finding the word "peas" in his mouth*) Sorry, peas?

JANE (*without breaking stride*) Little green vegetable.

ARTHUR Ah yes. Peas.

He watches television. He laughs.

It is good, this. It's very funny.

Have you seen it?

JANE Yes, Arthur. I've seen it.

JANE *sits down next to* ARTHUR *with her tea in her hand. She closes her eyes. When* ARTHUR *laughs abruptly, it makes her jump, she spills her tea.*

Oh for God's sake, Arthur!

ARTHUR *looks concerned.*

Sorry. It's ok, Arthur, my fault. It's just tea. I'll clean it up. My fault.

We watch her get a cloth and scrub the chair. ARTHUR *watches her and then turns his attention back to the television. She comes and sits down next to him, noticeably upset.*

ARTHUR *looks at her.*

ARTHUR You're upset.

JANE Oh. It's fine.

It's just...what the doctor said.

In a few years, you're not going to recognise me at all.

ARTHUR (*shocked but laughing*) NO! Wow... Well, that's a bit shit, isn't it? Why didn't he tell me that?

JANE He did, he did tell you.

ARTHUR When?

JANE But that's ok. You forget about it. You're...allowed to forget about it.

JANE *settles into her chair. Canned laughter is heard from the television. She settles in. A moment. We then snap out of State 2 and into State 1.*

I hate this bit

ARTHUR Me too.

Come on. Let's have a bit of music, eh?

Music magically comes on. **"YOU'RE NOBODY TILL SOMEBODY LOVES YOU"*** *– Dean Martin.* ARTHUR *strips for* JANE, *making her laugh. He places clothes around the room as music plays.* JANE *gets name tags from the chairs. When* ARTHUR *is in shirt, pants and socks, he and* JANE *meet centre stage and put sticky name tags on one another.*

JANE *bends over to pick up a shoe.*

Music cuts out as they age instantly and are back in flashback. They are old. State 2.

---

* For further information, please see Music Use Note on page v.

Stage 6: Severe Decline

JANE turns around after picking up ARTHUR's clothes strewn all over the floor. She is overwhelmed with relief that he is back.

JANE Oh, thank God! Arthur, where have you been? You scared me, going wandering dressed like that. What are we going to do with you, hey?

He is still staring blankly but cheerfully at her.

ARTHUR I thought she was in pain so I went to help her.

This hallucination has happened before. JANE knows this and is playing along.

JANE Right well, I hope she's ok now.

ARTHUR Have you seen her?

JANE No, sorry, I haven't.

ARTHUR I hope she's ok. She came in through the back door. We really should go back out and look for her, she looked upset.

JANE *(remaining calm)* Well, that's very nice of you to be showing so much concern, but I think it's fine.

ARTHUR She didn't look fine, you know.

JANE If she's not back soon, we'll go out and look for her. I'll make you a nice cup of tea, how does that sound?

Silence as she ushers him to sit down.

ARTHUR Ok, yes, yes ok.

Silence as he watches her and she sits him down and fusses over him.

Have I seen you round here many times before?

Looks at name tag.

Jane.

JANE *(without breaking stride)* Yes. Yes, I'm here quite often, Arthur.

ARTHUR Well, I can't have really seen you too many times.

JANE And why do you think that,/ Arthur?

ARTHUR Well, I'd most definitely remember you. I always remember the pretty ones.

JANE That's very kind of you. *(smiles at the part of her husband she recognises)* You're not looking too shabby yourself.

ARTHUR Thank you.

Does that mean you're staying here tonight?

JANE *(allowing another smile)* I think I am, yes.

ARTHUR Wow!

Silence as **ARTHUR** *mulls something over in his head.*

Are you sure you haven't seen her? Because she was definitely in here before.

JANE Yes. I'm sure, I didn't see her.

Tea! Tea. I was going to make you some tea, Arthur. I'll do that now, shall I?

ARTHUR *(becoming slightly suspicious)* Just seems strange that you didn't see—

JANE We've talked about this, Arthur, and we can go and look for her later, ok.

ARTHUR Why would you say later, we should go now!!

JANE *(momentary frustration)* That's enough about her now, ok!

What kind of tea would you like? Earl Grey? One of those funny green ones?

ARTHUR What have you done with her?

JANE Arthur, I haven't done anything – it's ok.

ARTHUR Don't deny it! I know you're lying, so don't deny it. Where is she?

JANE *(slightly panicky now)* Shall I take you through to the kitchen...

ARTHUR Don't, don't you dare take me anywhere!!

State 3 begins to build.

JANE It's ok, I'll get you a glass of water/ and you can—

ARTHUR NO! Don't you get me anything!

JANE I'm just going to get you a nice glass of water to/ cool you down—

ARTHUR *(becoming increasingly terrified)* Don't get me anything! Stay away from me.

JANE Arthur, it's ok, I'm here to look after you, no one is trying to hurt you *(walking towards* ARTHUR*)*.

ARTHUR *is cowering on the floor.*

ARTHUR I SAID STAY AWAY!

State 3 is almost unbearably loud. We are inside ARTHUR*'s head.*

JANE It's ok Arthur, I'm not here to hurt you, you know that, don't you?

ARTHUR What are you trying to do to me?

State 3 cuts out. JANE *is, sympathetic and concerned.*

JANE *(extremely upset but trying to keep controlled)* I'm just here to help you. Please know that.

ARTHUR *is muttering and cowering in the corner.*

JANE *is despairing. She takes a step towards him and he panics even more.*

*She eventually walks over to the CD player and this time she puts Frank Sinatra's **"FLY ME TO THE MOON"***, on out of desperation more than anything else.*

ARTHUR *slowly gets up, calming down instantly, and with a pained expression on his face walks/bobs over to her, grabs her hands and they begin to dance.*

ARTHUR *then begins to sing. We let this happen for a while. Let them dance, let him sing. He lets a pained groan come out of his mouth. As if this is the real **ARTHUR** underneath, struggling to get through.*

ARTHUR *begins to smile as if remembering something funny – he has his eyes closed, listening. Hands moving, fingers dancing, remembering.*

ARTHUR Red...red, yes it was...

JANE *is slightly confused and unable to comprehend what she might be about to hear.*

JANE What, Arthur? What are you trying to say...red what?

ARTHUR The...the...first time—

He laughs.

I'm sorry.

JANE Why? You don't have to be sorry about anything.

ARTHUR Yes, I am sorry.

He laughs.

I spilled red wine – on...

JANE *is overcome with this.*

It was all part of my plan

---

* For further information, please see Music Use Note on page v.

JANE Yes...yes, it was.

ARTHUR I asked you to dance...

This...music. Beautiful.

ARTHUR *continues to sing.*

I love you.

JANE I love you.

They continue to dance.

Music cuts out. We snap to State 1.

Those moments. Those tiny moments that have to fight so incredibly hard just to get through. Just to surface long enough for a smile of recognition or, or a song.

They made it all worthwhile.

Allows herself a small laugh.

I'd never liked his singing, but I think vright then it was simultaneously the most beautiful and most heartbreaking sound I ever heard.

I spent a lot of time thinking about memories. Unavoidable, I think. How much of your self is bound up in them. How empty you feel when there are none left.

It's strange which ones you hold on to.

Pause. She looks at ARTHUR *who is standing by the chair. By this point he has got changed into what he was wearing at the start, and so has she.*

ARTHUR *sits in his chair, youthful. They share a moment.*

We have reached the same image as the very first scene, with JANE's *head on* ARTHUR's *knee. They are old.*

Stage 7: Very Severe Decline

State 2:

JANE *rouses herself and checks her watch.*

JANE Time to go, Arthur, come on.

*As she helps **ARTHUR** up he panics and coughs, expressing his distress without words, gripping the arm of the chair. **JANE** tries to calm him but to no avail. She takes an iPod from her pocket and puts the headphones in **ARTHUR**'s ears and hits play. "FLY ME TO THE MOON"* bleeds from the headphones. **ARTHUR** calms and starts to make sounds to the music. He looks up, recognising **JANE**.*

She smiles.

Blackout.

---

* For further information, please see Music Use Note on page v.

VISIT THE SAMUEL FRENCH BOOKSHOP AT THE ROYAL COURT THEATRE

Browse plays and theatre books, get expert advice and enjoy a coffee

Samuel French Bookshop
Royal Court Theatre
Sloane Square
London
SW1W 8AS
020 7565 5024

Shop from thousands of titles on our website

 samuelfrench.co.uk

 samuelfrenchltd

 samuel french uk

Lightning Source UK Ltd.
Milton Keynes UK
UKHW010047240119
336085UK00005B/547/P